What My Christian Mother Never Told Me About Being a Teenager

What My Christian Mother Never Told Me About Being a Teenager

❧

A TEEN'S GUIDE TO: KNOWING GOD'S LOVE IN THE CHALLENGES WE FACE

Envi Cole

DEDICATION

This book is dedicated to my amazing husband
and our wonderful children. Through you,
God has given me the opportunity to walk in
my destiny.
Thank You!

Acknowledgements

To God Almighty, I acknowledge your presence in my life. Thank you for entrusting me with promoting the gospel and for giving me an opportunity to reach the beautiful and talented young minds that will change and transform the future. I will never share your glory and it is truly by grace that I am able to contribute in whatever small way. Thank you for beautifying my life and I don't take it lightly.

To my parents, I am truly your child and to my mother especially, you did the best you could with the tools you had as you raised us, giving up all of yourself so your children can have a better life. I love you so much. Thank you for always giving your best and for never giving up on any of your children.

To my husband, you are a true gift from God. You are the epitome of who and what a husband and father is, to me and to our children. Because of you, our children see how a father is supposed to care for his children and how a husband is supposed to care for his wife. I thank you for pushing me to pursue my goals.

To our children, God bless you. It is because of you that this goal has come to pass. You bring us so much joy and you all have taught us a lot about humility. Each of you have a special gift and you are unique in your own way. You will change the world for God.

To the men and women that have invested into my life in ministry and beyond, the Late Pastor Eustace Okoeka and his wife Pastor Famesha Okoeka, Pastor Brickson Sam and First Lady Annie Sam, Pastor Robyn Gool and First Lady Dr. Marilyn Gool and so many more that have contributed to my Spiritual growth, thank you.. I have grown Spiritually in part, because of your investment knowingly or unknowingly. Your labor in the Lord is not in vain.

Finally, If I have come across your path, it is not by mere chance. To my friends and family, you have contributed to my life in many ways, I thank you for the lessons you taught me.

CONTENTS

Dedication   v

Acknowledgements   vii

One
How Do You See Yourself?   1

Two
Acceptance By Others   7

Three
Stress And Time Management   13

Four
Peer Pressure And Expectations By Others   16

Five
Mental And Physical Health Issues   19

Six
Positive Role Models And Heroes   25

Seven
Temptation With Drugs And Alcohol   28

Eight
Onscreen Violence And Unhealthy Social Media   32

Nine
Bullying On And Offline   35

Ten
Risky Sexual Activity And Behavior   37

Eleven
Well, Everyone Is Doing It!   42

Twelve
God Sees Everything I Do   46

Thirteen
Sexually Transmitted Infections   49

Fourteen
God Is Love   51

Fifteen
"I Commit"   55

About The Author   57
References   59

One

~

How do you see yourself?

In Proverbs 23:7 (NLT), we read that as a man thinks in his heart, so is he. This shows that your perception is important. Having the right perception about yourself is necessary as your teenage years can be both awesome but also filled with challenges. How teens view themselves can have different outcomes, both positive and negative. One's self image can be influenced by their peers or what they see in the media, although it is supposed to be built from within and from God's word. For this reason, it is important that the image you have of yourself as a teen or preteen is shaped from within. Are you feeling bad about yourself because you think you don't measure up to your peers or do you feel that if you don't do what they do, they will reject you?

These are legitimate concerns and when you know who you are and more importantly, whose you are, it will change your perception about yourself in a positive way. You must be persuaded about who God is and the part he plays or is suppose to play in your life. It is important to see yourself from God's perspective and to remember that

"God created human beings in his own image" (Genesis 1:27, NLT) and that his image is on you. See yourself that way! Do not let the world shape how you see yourself and only proclaim what you desire in a positive way. Do not tell yourself that you are ugly or that you are not enough. Instead, look in the mirror and tell yourself that "God's image is on me". When you are having a bad thought about how you see yourself, tell yourself positive things you what to see about your body, your life and your future, not what you currently see, that is negative.

These positive affirmations can boost your confidence greatly. Imagine, walking in the consciousness that the image of the creator, God almighty, is on you. The image of "I AM", the image of the maker of the universe, the image of the one who will never leave you nor forsake you, the image of the one who goes before you, making every crooked place straight, yes, his image is on you. It takes practice and it will also help you build resilience in your emotions when you continue to tell yourself what the bible says about you and when you believe it. I hear a lot of teens say, but "I just don't see myself" that way and they think they are lying to themselves. What you feed in your life and in your Spirit is what grows. Build your perception about yourself from what the Bible says about you and make faith confessions instead of acting on how you feel. By this I mean, when you feel down or sad or depressed for instance, don't act out that sadness, tell yourself how you want to feel (for instance, say I am strong, I have a lot of energy and act that out). A strong person doesn't stay in bed, in the dark all day. Get up, say boldly that you are strong and show it. Think about whose image is on you and know you are reflecting that image.

Even as an adult, you are going to find out that perception is important. Now that I have the tools the Bible brings me, I tell myself that "the Spirit God gave us does not make us timid, but gives us power, love and self-discipline" (2 Timothy 1:7, NLT). Know it takes practice and as you tell yourself more and more, what the bible says about you, you will begin to believe and own those words for yourself. It will be difficult for a person who always tell themselves negative things, to be upbeat and stay in a great mood. Ok, what if as you read this book you say I don't even know God, I don't believe in him, etc. Well, I challenge you to give God and the Bible a chance. Investigate knowing him for yourself by reading his word and asking him to come into your heart and to help you in your teenage years to make good choices and to walk in the inheritance he has already given you and provided for you. Do not Judge him based on the Christians you know, have a personal relationship with him as your Lord and Savior and see your life transform.

If I tell myself I'm going to have an amazing day, no matter what happens that day, I can look at the amazing parts of it, always looking at the glass as half full than half empty and if I do an inventory, I can see that what I proclaim about that day, will be more of what I see, and accept into my Spirit. Our words have power and it is important that we watch your words. What you give the universe is what the universe can work with. If you tell yourself positives things, you can't help but have positive words in the universe to work on your behalf. I remember my daughter as a young teen, put her fears and goals on her bedroom wall. With revelation in prayer, one day she was away at school and the Holy Spirit placed on my heart to remove the section of every fear she had written on her wall. Remember what 2 Timothy 1:7 says.

I had seen those fears on her wall for at least a few days and know that the human mind is prone to act by emotions, which is a real part of us, although we should not merely live by our emotions. She had practical things on that list like spiders and snakes but as a Christian, always profess what the bible says about you. It doesn't mean you dismiss your emotions because if they were not important, God would not have given them to us. If they were not important, the enemy, satan, would not try to use our emotions against us.

Say for instance, someone say all of the time that he or she is great. After some time, they will begin to believe that they are great. They may even go further and investigate, what it means to be great and do their part, in an attempt to achieve greatness. Your Spirit works to produce what comes out of your mouth, and you should say good and positive things if you want to have a positive perspective about yourself. When you have a positive self image, you will follow them with actions to see that image manifest in everything you do. Even if you are not great now, it gives you a goal to work towards. Feed yourself with positive words and feed your Spirit with words that help you see yourself as God sees you.

As the bible says, you are the Salt of the earth, you are blessed to be a blessing, you are above and not beneath. We cannot go by how you feel because feelings can get you in trouble and cause you to make wrong decisions. I may not feel like going to work but I go because I know it is the right choice as I am required to show up if I want to be employed by that establishment, among so many important reasons. I may not feel like going to church but I go because I know that is my feeding ground where I get my instructions from God through my Pastor, whom God has given me after his heart to instruct me in the things of God. Building a positive mental and body image takes work and practice.

If you are having any challenge in this area or ever feel like you don't measure up, ask God to help you by praying and also know that you have to do your part. In every area of life, we have a responsibility in getting the outcomes we want. Merely believing something will happen is not enough. Focus on things that will help you make good choices like hanging out with positive people, people with positive body image and by telling yourself positive and good things, even if that is not how you currently feel. You are enough and you deserve the most amazing life that God envisions and has purposed for you.

"My Christian mother never told me "Self image should come from within, so invest positivity into yourself"

Two

～

Acceptance by Others

Teens, like most people, want to be accepted by their families, friends and others they know. We want to know that we are wanted, needed and valued. As teens, you spend a great number of hours weekly, with your peers and you share your ideas, thoughts and experiences. As a Christian, God tells us in 2 Corinthians 6:17 (NLT) to "come out from among unbelievers, and separate yourselves from them. Don't touch their filthy things, and I will welcome you". This can be a great challenge for a Christian teen because as you value being accepted, it can be difficult to stand on your own. As you build capacity, the teen years is just the start, so you are learning and gaining the tools you need, to be able to challenge satan by what is written in the word of God and not just accept the lies and deception satan brings you.

Always remember that you are not here just to be accepted, although that is something we all want and we see examples of how even Jesus was favored by men. God did not intend for any of us to stand alone. Take for instance, Jesus had man's favor when he was helped by Simon to carry his cross. Jesus had 12 men that helped him in his ministry. Know that you are unique, with God's image on you and that being accepted should not be your priority. If we focus on being accepted, we can make negative choices because we want to be a part of the crowd. If acceptance is your priority, you will ignore that the crowd is making bad choices that will lead them to missing out on the amazing life that God intended for them. Take this scenario, a student (Jane) at your school, is making wrong choices and how she got here is another point all together. You can clearly see that Jane is drinking, sneaking out, she has a boyfriend that has introduced her using drugs and having sex and now her grades have dropped. This is clearly not a good example for you. Unfortunately, this student is on the basketball team and is popular, so everyone wants to be a part of her crowd. It is probably just a matter of time before things get completely out of control and Jane drops out of school and gets kicked off the basketball team.

Some of what is going on with this young lady, you may not even see or know but she seems like a pretty friendly and nice person and you may not think anything is wrong with being friends with her. I mean, she has a car, she picks you up to go to the mall and her mother actually listens to you, something you think you do not get in your own home. Despite this, people can only teach you what they know. I mean, I cannot teach you to be great and successful in your classes, when I am failing. Always remember that you are made in the image and likeness of God himself and you must give yourself boundaries and with God's help, you can have those boundaries with others.

Be careful and selective about what you accept into your soul, meaning through your eyes especially. When you think about wanting to be accepted, what do you do to show that God's image is on you? We cannot accept anything in our soul and Spirit, for the sake of being accepted. Even as an adult, it may shock you to know that adults need to have boundaries also, if they are going to make good choices, which you can also do as a teen! First, you have to decide within yourself that you are going to do so ahead of time and ask God to help you. This is why you are in a good place by reading this book. You are so loved by someone that they decided to give you this tool to help guide you. God gives us a choice to make the right choice so your parents can only guide you and give you tools. You have to say "NO" sometimes in life, so you don't say yes to everything.

If you do not decide in your heart ahead of time that you are not going to have sex before marriage for instance, then you open up yourself to doing so prematurely. When you decide ahead of time what you are not going to do, it is more likely that you will stick to your plans than when you leave things to chance. Know that you can asked God to help you make and keep those choices. If you decide ahead of time that you are not going to drink alcohol, it is likely that you will be more conscious about the places you go or the people you hang around. Joe says he's a Christian, but the true test is living a life that reflects the character of Christ. Believing in all of God's word as you see it in the bible (and following his word in your actions), pray to God and live a life that is pleasing to him. Christopher invites you to a party and says his friend Delvin will be brining lots of alcohol. Knowing you have purposed in your heart that you are not going to drink alcohol, you may have to make a decision that you are not going to that party so you do not open yourself up to drinking.

It seems innocent overall, I mean, you don't have to drink and you can just sit in a corner while everyone else is having fun. If drinking alcohol is the only way they consider having fun, you probably should say no and not go. This may be a more effective strategy than making a choice to go, being ignorant of the devices of the devil. The devil is not going to challenge where you are strong. Likely, it is going to be when you are in need, at your weakest hour. You are at the party, it is going well, you haven't touched alcohol and you tell yourself, "see, I have self control and I can overcome temptation". Then, you get a call from another friend, who doesn't even know where you are. She tells you about her issues and that changes your mood and you feel sad and down. Then, another friend who doesn't drink as far as you know, prompts you to try one small drink.

A small voice tells you no, remember what you told yourself you will not do? Despite this, you don't make any changes, you don't leave, the pressure mounts and you just want to raise your mood. You want to forget about your friend's issues, not knowing that by drinking you may be affecting your emotions and impair your judgement. You then say what the heck and make a choice you said you wouldn't. Just think of the possible consequences and it can become a habit. When you build your Spirit, you become more keen to the promptings of the Holy Spirit. Maybe, there was a small voice that told you not to go to the party but did you listen. God talks to you all the time and as you seek him and fellowship with him and surrenders to him, you can hear him more clearing and sense him in your Spirit. It may be the urge to not go to a party or not hang out with a certain friend or not exposing yourself to thing on the internet you thought was just out of curiosity. When you don't listen, you are actually opening your Spirit and your soul to things that you were not supposed to introduce your eyes to, like emotional garbage! There are things that God intended to be garbage and humans have fooled us to make us believe it is for entertainment.

Don't open up yourselves to these things. This is going to be key in protecting yourself from possible emotional pain. Choosing the places you go to, choosing what your eyes see and what you ultimately imprint into your Spirit, is important. Others may seem "cool" or seem to be part of the "it" crowd, but you have to see how their life is.

Are they respectful to their parents and others, are they doing well in school, do they lie and steal? Choose to be accepted and supported by people that are going to help lead you closer to God, not just those that are supportive and accepting of whatever is presented to them.

"My Christian mother never told me that God's image is on me"

Three

かく

Stress and time management

How you manage your time can have a great impact on what you can accomplish on a daily basis and ultimately, in life . It is easy for hours to slip by as you browse social media outlets, watch a video or two, while forgetting that 5 page paper due in 2 days. Time management is important and necessary in being productive. Unfortunately, you will find out if you do not master these skills during your teenage years, its only going to spill over into adulthood. Making a list and sticking to it is going to be helpful for some of you. As humans, we are not going to get it right all the time but having a plan gives you a better chance of following it than not having a plan.

If you do not have a plan, then you leave your life to chance and that can give you results you really do not want or consequences you did not intend. Give yourself time for what you want to accomplish for the day. For example, designate 1 hour for social medial for a specific day and you must move to the next task on the list when that hour is up by learning to be disciplined. It takes making choices and you can make good choices with God's help. Its like opening a pack of potato chips and eating from the bag. If we give ourselves unlimited options of how much we can eat, we may end up eating the whole bag in one seating, while if you portion out what you intend to eat, that gives you some boundaries about how much you actually consume. In life, we must learn to quench the appetites of the flesh. Yes, just because we have options and a choice doesn't mean we should exercise our choices. God gives us the choice to make a good choice. The bible says in Deuteronomy 30, 15-16 that "behold, I have set before you today life and prosperity, and death and evil. [16] For I command you today to love Yahweh your God, to walk in his ways and to keep his commandments, his statutes, and his ordinances, that you may live and multiply, and that Yahweh your God may bless you in the land where you go in to possess it". God is so awesome, he doesn't take away our appetites and our wants, he gives us the choice and tools to train our appetites. He doesn't take away your choices when you are a teenager, instead, this is a beautiful time to mold yourself in the way you want to see it later. You will find this also true that adults have some of the same challenges if we do not master our appetites in the beginning.

Train your eyes. Don't look at everything, don't listen to everything and anything, put up boundaries and learn to say no! You will hear experiences from your friends but curiosity is not necessarily good for you. You do not know what your friends are really into, therefore, when they bring ideas and new thoughts to you, think about your morals, values and beliefs and make sure they align. Be very careful of the voice that may say did the "Bible really say that", did my parents really say so, do my Pastor really believe that? The devil told Eve in the garden of Eden in Genesis 3:1(NLT), "did God really say you must not eat the fruit from any of the trees in the garden? This reminds us that satan tries to create doubt, in an attempt to steal your faith so you can miss your blessing from God.

He said to the woman, Did God REALLY say you must not eat

from any tree in the garden? That was not what God said but the devil will use what God says and present you with false information that look like truth because he's a fraud and an impersonator. God said for Adam and Eve not to eat of the tree of good and evil but hear what the devil told Adam and Eve instead. Deception is a key tool that the devil will use to get you to walk in error. Temptation starts in your heart and with the eyes. In your temptation, the devil will use deceptions, so train your eyes to focus on what you want and take it off things that will get you into trouble. Adults, like your parents and caregivers are quick to tell you about what they have scheduled, including their plans for you as their children. With this, unnecessary stress may be created simply because of what others expect from you. Do know they really have your best interest and mean well. They are put in your lives to guide and help teach you how to make good choices. Teenagers want to be accepted by peers and this can make it difficult to make healthy decisions about their plans and goals. When we manage our time wisely, it is a way to decrease stress that may be unnecessary. Sometimes planning wisely and being proactive can keep us calm, than when we waste our time and become overwhelmed, causing stress and other mental and physical issues in our lives.

"My Christian mother never told me "I can make healthy choices with God's help"

Four

~~

Peer Pressure and expectations by others

There are so many pressures put on teens from parents, society and by themselves. Despite this, know that "you got this". You really do! Take little bites and you will find out you can accomplish all the wonderful goals you set for yourself. This is going to take some discipline on your end and know you have a responsibility in the things you want to accomplish in life because there are things that others just cannot do for you. Just because you do not feel like getting out of bed, doesn't mean that you can't or shouldn't try to do so. I am not discrediting issues of sadness or depression etc. I understand the challenge you face but you must make a decision in your heart and your mind that you are going to try to make changes, even small changes towards progress and you can do it. There may be things outside of your control but there are things you can do and choices you can make. Parents have expectations for their teens regarding choices to shape their lives. We are not talking about unrealistic expectations from parents and sometimes their approach can cause more stress in you life. There are realistic expectations that can become overwhelming but you can learn to mange them appropriately.

We know it can be difficult at times and you may say that others do not understand what you are going through. Society has its own stresses and expectation it places on teens but know that God is on your side. He will not give you a burden you cannot carry. He's got your back. Keep your mind on him and he will help you make good choices and keep you in perfect peace. Surrendering to God is going to be what gives him control and permission to help you. God doesn't force you but we cannot want to have our own way and live our lives how we want to, and think God is in control of the areas in our lives we refuse to give him control of. Your life does not have to be a life of ups and downs, it really can be beautiful and your teenage years can be pleasant. Surrender yourself to God and he will make it beautiful. Turn to God for strength and power. Don't allow just anything into your imagination because it can have an effect on how you think and perceive things. We understand that expectations and pressure from your peers to conform to what they want you to be, can be overwhelming. Despite this, know ahead of time that you are perfect in God's eyes and that you do not have to be like others and even fulfill the expectations of others. Make it your goal to be like Jesus, not like your peers.

"My Christian mother never told me "I can manage expectations in a healthy way"

Five

~~~

Mental and physical health issues

March to the drumbeat of God! As a child of God, we must know we do not have to accept whatever the enemy brings us. By this, know when you surrender to God, your life is not just random in the things that happens to you. If u begin to not listen to your parents, u may start making choices that can lead to negative consequences. The bible gives us the prescription to long life in saying to honor your mother and father if you want to live long. As a teenager, learn to make good choices early and learn to respect those that are in a position of authority over your life.

Many people face physical and mental health issues. Grant it, there are genetic predispositions but know that is not a life or death sentence. It gives you a sneak peak or an insight into how you can better manage your choices at times. Yes, there are things you cannot control. A person who has a family history of high blood pressure may have an advantage early to make lifestyle changes that can de-

crease their chances of having the same health problem and consequences. Yes, there are things we can and cannot control. Don't
think you do not have choices. I know that predispositions and family history can play a part in many ways in people's lives, but it is not
necessarily how the story ends for you also. Predisposition to mental
health challenges may mean that one cannot partake in lifestyle
choices that another teen may partake of and be able to cope. There
are a lot of good people who have had a lot of bad things happen to
them. They may have been exposed to experiences they do not deserve. I get it! You have authority, yes, there are things that are genetic that want to dictate our future, but you do not have to accept
what the enemy tries to bring you. A teenager that has a predisposition to mental illness may give themselves a real change at mental illness if they make certain choices.

We cannot do what everyone is doing. Some people may not see
their predispositions manifest, until they make a choice. A predisposition to alcoholism is not going to affect someone that does not
drink alcohol. That person will have to bring alcohol into their body.
Therefore, we need to be mindful. Do not accept the labels people
put on you. Reject negativity into your Spirit. You can talk to God
yourself and ask him to help you make good choices. You can reject
things from entering into your thoughts, your emotions and your
Spirit. Just because the doctor or your mother says you have a mental
illness, doesn't mean it is a life sentence. I am not talking about denial
and what the facts are but counteract what the enemy is bringing you
by what the word of God says about you. The bible says that by the
stripes of Jesus, we are healed. So if you are healed (believing God's
word), how do you negotiate your body or your mind not working at
optimum health, with what God says about sickness and disease. Yes, I
do believe in science. I hear young people say for instance, I can't help
it, i'm bipolar or I have OCD or anger problems or whatever else they
have been diagnosed with. How you feel or what you have been diag-

nosed with is not a free pass to not be accountable nor is it a crutch. Mental illness is real and you can manage it appropriately with following the plan that your medical and psychiatric professionals have in place. God has given them the wisdom to assist in dealing with health issues. You are blessed in the city, you are blessed in the field, you shall live and not die, you are above and not beneath, God has not given you a Spirit of fear, but a Spirit of love, power and a sound mind, and know that Jesus came to give you life in abundance. When you say these words, your body will align with your Spirit. Proclaim what the bible says about you, and do your part. Yes, you may be doing this while following the advice of medical professionals which may include medication or surgery and God's word until you see the change you want to see, don't give up. God may even rectify the situation in the midst of your medical intervention but you do your part until you no longer need the medication or whatever treatment your doctor has prescribed. Remember, you have a responsibility and you must be accountable and own the part you play in your own life.

It doesn't mean you don't follow doctor's orders or you do not seek medical attention, it means that even in the challenges you face, you speak what the Bible says about you and use wisdom, as you navigate the world. You may have be on medication for bipolar disorder, as you take that medication, you tell yourself that bipolar does not have control over you, you speak good things over your emotions. You tell yourself that you have a sound mind as you ask God to help you manage the extreme emotions you are feeling. Tell yourself you resist depression and that you resist mood swings. You do not hang around people who cannot control their own emotions. You become mindful about your environment.

Only God can take away the pains of the past. I tell teenagers on a regular basis that we cannot change our past as we all may know. Sometimes we open doors to the enemy and then when things go wrong we want to ask God why and blame God. I hear teenagers tell me they don't believe in God, they investigate witchcraft and other areas that's not of God and is not intended by God and then wonder why the enemy is tormenting them. Many of them do not understand the Spirit world at their age, and do not know the consequences of investigating demonic activity. They cannot focus on, or accept the beautiful life that God has set before them. Surender to God and he will make your life more beautiful. What do you tell a teen who has lost a parent to death or divorce at a young age and is now depressed. Yes, they have every reason to be sad and depressed by the world's view. Regardless of this, they do not have to stay depressed.

Although you do not dismiss your emotions, acknowledge how you feel and know that you do not have to stay in a rot. You may feel anger and want to question God, but the bible says in Ephesians 4:26 that "in your anger, do not sin" (NLT). Do not let the sun go down while you are still angry". God does not want you to dismiss your emotions, he gave them to you. However, process that emotion, then move quickly from an emotion that is causing you problems to a more positive emotion. If you are angry, don't stay angry. Learn to process your feelings with adults that care about you and always have someone you trust in a healthy way. You may look around and say "I do not have that person right now" but that is the reason you have an opportunity to find someone.

You may have that person already but have never thought about if you really trust them. Make sure it is an adult. I know it is easy to say that you trust your friend but as passengers in the same boat, we need to look up to someone who has more depth in their training. A captain of a ship for instance, is a better person to get us to our destination because he or she has the training than a passenger, who is just on the ship for a fun ride. Our friends may seem to understand us better but we have to be mindful and understand that they may not have had an opportunity to gain the tools needed to lead you. As a teenager, you are smart and talented and I cannot take that away from you. Despite this, know that adults generally have had more experiences and God placed your parents in your path to lead and help teach you about how to make good choices.

Sometimes, teens may look to their friends as supportive because they feel like they will not be judged by them. Do expect your parents and adult mother and father figures that God has put in your life to hold you accountable, in an attempt to ensure that you are on the right path in life. Sometimes, we want to run away from them because we do not want to be corrected but God wants them to correct you. I am not talking about an abusive situation but truly a situation that parents and caregivers are using to care and groom you for a better future. Just because you do not like rules, doesn't make your parents and caregivers are abusive or bad people. If you knew everything, you would not need instruction in school or college or at home. Resist pride at an early age and know you need instruction and God's help. To get this help, God has placed people in your lives to guide you.

As I tell young people regularly, bad things they do not deserve may have happened to them but God can change their lives. In order to have a different result, we must make a decision to do things differently. It is important to accept that you past happened and embrace that it has helped shaped you to this point. Then, let go of the negativity, forgive your aggressors and ask God to heal your heart from the pain. In addition, do not expose yourself to risky behavior. In doing so, you are helping to decrease your risk for mental and physical health issues. For instance, many teens struggle with their weight and this can have an impact on their body image, and may lead to other problems.

As a teen, it is important to train your appetites, as you will need to do, even as an adult. By this, I mean moderate what you do and don't just eat anything, don't watch just anything, don't go just anywhere, don't do just anything. Give yourself boundaries and listen to that small voice that tells you positive things. Play it safe always. For instance, by going to a random party not knowing what type of people or activities will be available, you open yourself to making mistakes and getting involved in activities you didn't intend to involve in. Even the exposure to activities that are not in line with God's word, becomes a gateway to imprint negativity into your Spirit. If you go to a place where everyone is smoking, this may expose you to wanting to try smoking, not knowing that whatever you are being offered may be laced with something else you didn't bargain for. I have seen many many teens that smoked marijuana, had it in edible form or offered some other illicit product. Then they begin to hallucinate, become manic or psychotic and paranoid.

They may have been predisposed to mental illness but if they never exposed themselves to drugs, they may not be in the position they are in. Mental health issues are real. I remember a family member who always end up being paranoid after he indulges in drug use. Then the parents ask and want the doctors to have all the answers. Everything is not as a result from inside your brain, we have to be accountable for the part we play in our own health and our own lives. Sometimes, mental and physical health issues are induced by choices we have made and what we have introduced into our bodies. Despite this, God can change your life, no matter what choices you have made, God is not trying to punish you for being bad. He came to give you life in abundance, therefore walk in that consciousness.

"My Christian mother never told me "my choices can lead to poor mental health"

Six

~

Positive role models and heroes

Lacking good mentors, role models and heroes can have a detrimental effect on a teenager's self esteem and confidence. Children model what they see. Parents can only teach their children what they know and what children see is what they are going to model. What you do in the home, as well as what you tell them has to be consistent. When parents tell their children that they have to use their time wisely, they need to show that consistency as parents, in their actions and need to be good role models. Children have grown up in situations that can really challenge a child's sense of security. A mother that abuses her children and leave them in unhealthy situations, or a child becoming a parent as a teenager, and out of wedlock, many through no fault of their own, are circumstances that threatens a teenager's sense of security. So many good young people have fallen into the trap of the enemy knowingly and unknowingly. They may have been exposed to situations that no child should be the subject to. Despite this, know that God is always with you.

Sometimes, children and teens lose role models to divorce, death and other circumstances that are beyond their control. Some years back, it was difficult for my own children, after their father was no longer living with us, as a result of our divorce. I believe that divorce is not the perfect plan for families and that God want families to stay together. Despite this, in Matthew 19:8 (NLT) Jesus replied, "Moses permitted divorce only as a concession to your hard hearts, but it was not what God had originally intended. It was not easy for them but know that time truly heals. When there is a change in the home and family structure, children may blame themselves and question what they did wrong. However, know that you cannot blame yourself for situations that are out of your control and know that adults have to own their choices and ensure that regardless of the circumstance with your parents, you do not lose your self worth. No matter what you are going through, you are loved by God.

No matter the circumstance, even if it is a good situation like "dad moved to go to work", it can still be difficult for teens to cope when a parent is out of the home. Recently, a family friend passed away leaving behind small children. Just image what they are going through and the possible consequences of their father not being a part of their lives. First, know that your pain is valid. Despite this, no matter what grief or circumstance we face in life, know that God is our ultimate role model. Know he will never leave you or forsake you. There are things we cannot understand or deserve and it is not for us to judge the reason why it happens. Do not blame yourself, do not question God and do not hold on to that pain. Only God truly understand and can relieve that pain. Yes, you are entitled to your emotions, sometimes the pains you feel may come from people you love that have disappointed and hurt you. You may have "lost" people you are close to through death, divorce or just due to a friendship that went sour or just wasn't meant to be. It hurts, Please remember that only God can take away our pain. When bad things happen, people want to hold God responsible and ignore the wicked devil, satan, who is always wanting to resist you in all things.

Shattered Dreams (embrace your pain and let it go)

The hurt and the tears and the pain we feel
The pain is not isolated for it is "our Pain"
We feel the sorrow and anger and grief
Those that have gone, we long for their touch

Dust, dust, dust from where they came
Grief and pain, tries to destroy us
We remember the Dreams and visions for "us"
but it only causes more pain Yes, a deep pain

One that penetrates our very soul
For the connection with loved ones was severed all in a moment
It fills us with questions, sometimes anger and rage
Yet we hope to hear their words

We remember their pain, our pain
It makes us want justice, but from who
If you act out of rage, then you cause more pain
Rest in the Lord and remember vengeance is his

"My Christian mother never told me "God is my role model"

Seven

⌘

Temptation with drugs and alcohol

There are so many temptations, especially as a teenager because the devil do not want you to walk in your destiny. Satan does not want you to fulfill the plans that God has for you, so what better way to derail those plans than when you are a teenage. Alcohol and drugs lower your inhibitions and can expose you to things and choices you did not intend to be a part of. The choices you make are going to have an impact on your life. As teenagers, you are at a point in your life where you have more independence and your parents are not always going to be there with you and to tell you what to do and not do. Temptations may be a constant challenge for people . There may be areas in your life you feel you have no control over and when you have a thought about it, you have to follow through with what your mind tells you to do. In Mark 14:38, (NLT) the bible says "watch and pray so that you will not fall into temptation, the Spirit is willing but the flesh is weak" and know with God's help, things that used to be difficult, you will find that they will become easy.

People may make it seem as if there is no pleasure in sin but many sinful activities can be enjoyable though the consequences are not. The Bible says we should renew our minds, therefore, you cannot expose and indulge in everything that feels good, there are consequences. Don't expose your eyes to everything. From the beginning, we see Adam and Eve faced temptation and even Jesus. After fasting for 40 days, we see the devil tempted him, not when Jesus was at his best, but when he was in need. He had fasted for 40 days and so the devil knew that and tempted him when he was in need. He was hungry, at least the devil thought so and asked Jesus to turn stone into bread. Why would bread be important after no food for 40 days? Pay attention and you will see that temptations do not really look as attractive when you are mentally in a good place, it looks more attractive when you are in need. Jesus was in need. For instance, you may feel down or sad and that may be the time you get a call from a friend to go to a party. You know you should not go but a small voice tells you it may make you feel better.

Know the word of God and you will be able to tell the devil "it is written". The devil is no fool and he comes in your time of need and desperation but not to help you, but to tempt you to try to lead you out of the will of God for your life. That first bottle of alcohol can become a stronghold and now you may not know how to stop. This can lead to not focusing in school anymore, maybe resulting in you dropping out or not go to college. Just imagine if your goal was to become a physician, how can you accomplish that without going through the process, which includes medical school. These are ways the devil gains access into your life so do not give him the opportunity. A friend may say they smoke marijuana because it helps them focus but as a result, they have been skipping school and making other bad choices. On the surface, what may seem like help, is merely an open door for satan to mess up our lives so we must not give him that opportunity. That friend that smokes may not be able to keep up with his or her school work because what started as an innocent activity with friends has now become maladaptive, keeping him or her from pursuing goal and dreams because smoking has taken over that person's live.

"My Christian mother never told me just a taste is an open door"

Eight

〜

Onscreen violence and unhealthy social media

A teenager finds out that a so called friend is talking negatively about her on social media. So, she takes a hammer to the friend's house and hits her on the head, true story. It is important to know that television is not reality. The bible says train up a child in the way that he should go and when he is older, he will not depart from it. It is important to get instruction from your home and to use the instructions that your parents give you. Some may say, I don't have a parent or role model I look up to. God's word says, I put before you life and death, choose life. Sometimes those choices may mean not having a social media page or to limit certain friends from your social media. When you find out someone is talking badly about you, what can you do about it in a healthy way? You can unfriend that person, delete your social media page or limit your involvement, tell them how they made you feel in a respective way, build resilience so you can bounce back quickly from that situation and have healthy coping skills for when you are not in a good place emotionally. Your parents are not going to always be there to check your apps or to check your phones. Tell God and yourself you will live for him. You have to renew your mind daily with prayer and doing what you know is right, using the Bible as your guide. You may really not want to go to a specific place but because of peer pressure, AKA, the devil creating an opportunity to set you up to make a bad choice, you may choose to go. Living your life for God is not a difficult choice and you can have a beautiful life in God.

Social media has been a good platform to connect with friends and family and it can be used for good reasons and with good outcomes. Despite this, it has become an area where people compete or present false realities or to get other peoples' attention. Think about this and with five million or even five followers telling someone what you should do, one can be influenced by social medial if it is not used for the purpose it is intended. There needs to be a healthy balance. Limit the amount of time you spend on social media and have healthy and other ways to interact with your friends and family. Sometimes, you may not even know a person well and just because you go to the same school or church, you may think you should be friends on social media platforms then find out it is not a good choice.

There are so many shows and movies that can expose you to violence which can make you get used to it and think it is not a big deal. Although your parents and role models are in your life to guide you, as a teenager, many times, you are trusted. You therefore have to do and watch what is appropriate television shows that are healthy for your emotions. Many television shows may seem innocent on the surface but take for instance a teen that is emotionally not in a good place and watching shows with a lot of violence, that TV programs may not help the situation. Therefore, monitor what you expose your eyes to on television and in person. Anything you let go through your eyes, has an opportunity to get imprinted into your soul so leave good imprints on your soul.

With movies and shows needing to create more and more shock value onscreen, we see that the story lines can include excessive violence. Even with ratings shown to allow viewers to know what age group should be watching the content, we can easily see that there are times when there is excessive violence presented for a certain age group. You do not want to continue to introduce your eyes to such experiences. It can create an opportunity to want to copy what you have seen or want to create an experience like you have seen. It can be a gateway to rob your mind of it's innocence and introduce content that is not meant to build you up but to give you options of violence.

"My christian mother never told me that the eyes are the windows to the soul"

Nine

∾

Bullying on and offline

As we all may know, kids can be insensitive and down right mean to one another although they may not know how it makes other people feel. Social media has just given some an opportunity to extend their bullying platforms. Know your self worth and protect yourself mentally. Sometimes it is better to be proactive than to be reactive. Therefore, realize you do not need to do what you see others do. Know you have intrinsic value. If you didn't know this, please do so today that people will tell you who you're supposed to be, if you do not know who you are. Let this be imprinted in your spirit. Children will always find a reason to bully others. They say offense is not given, offense is taken. Your peers may not like that you are Christian, or they may think you don't have nice clothes or reject you for no reason. Some kids will always find a reason to pick on someone whether you let them or not. We cannot control what others do, we can only control our response. A bully has issues with him or herself and if anyone needs to minimize or discredit you so they can seem relevant, they have a problem, not you.

Despite this, you have to realize that If you do not know your value, then you give the bully power to torment and upset you and that is not God's plan for your life. The enemy is looking for any opening to discredit you, to belittle you, bully you and there are spirits that work behind the scenes, using those who bully others, to push satan's agenda forward. Bullying can make someone's self esteem low, they may interrupt their education and end up being home schooled because they have become so anxious about going to school and face their bully. This may lead to other challenges. Know, it is ok to tell a bully that you do not like how he or she makes you feel. In addition, let school authorities, as well as your caregivers know what is going on at school so they can come up with a plan to resolve the situation appropriately. Remember the story mentioned earlier about the girl with the hammer? She found out through a friend that she was being bullied on social media, and went to the bully's house with a hammer and assaulted her. She stated she thought about setting the bully's house on fire but didn't.

She hit the bully with the hammer. Now, there is not justification for bullying and what if the assault had resulted in the person being bullied, getting hurt really bad. I remember a true story about a young man that punched another person, one punch, the person fell, hit their head and ended up dying. Yes, one punch! That resulted in that young man going to prison for an extended amount of time. Although to you, it may seem justified, you do not get to choose your consequences for your actions so we must be careful. There is always a way to deal with a situation appropriately. This is why it is important to train your appetite. Every one wants to be on social media and this can give you a false sense of reality about yourself and others.

"My Christian mother never told me "just because I can, doesn't mean I should"

Ten

∾

risky sexual activity and behavior

Don't use your body as a house of fun but see it as God intended. Your body is God's temple and the Holy Spirit lives in you. God is so loving and kind that he provided his Holy word to instruct us for our own benefit. You may know about the 10 commandments and let's take "thou shalt not commit adultery" and the verse in the bible that states, let every man have his own wife. These two examples gives us insight into God's intention for one man to be with one woman and one woman for one man. This is so important because if you do not realize why you should save yourself for the one person that God has destined for you, you will not have a reason to do so. The bible says that people perish because of a lack of knowledge and you have the opportunity to be enlightened.

Marriage is the most sacred relationship you will enter and sex is a sacred gift from God. God has given us every instruction in his word concerning life and Godliness. Some may think there is nothing wrong with giving yourselves away to anyone who wants you. Well, there are so much practical problems with that. A teen told me recently, "I remember the guy I lost my virginity to, I went to see him one day and there was another girl at his house and she was expecting a baby. Just think how an 18 year old who has got a lot to learn can deal with such heartbreak. God is really trying to guard us from such heart aches and therefore, he gives us a roadmap with road blocks. We have an amazing gift of choice but we must know we do not have a choice to change the consequences for our choices. The Bibles states, I put before you life and death, choose life. After that situation, the young lady stated she really didn't know how to process what just happened. A kind hearted girl stopped by her boyfriend's house to drop off a birthday gift and now scarred. How can a heart move on. She had just given something so sacred to someone so undeserving. The only one deserving of your virginity is one who has made a commitment in marriage. Isn't God awesome to want to protect you as his child.

As we all know, children need boundaries and instructions. No matter how mature we are, we can walk in error so he safeguards us by stopping us from making silly mistakes that could cost us in the future. Unless you have made up your mind ahead of time, then you open yourself to risky behavior. The enemy does not want you to know that your virginity is sacred and that sex is sacred and wants you to give yourself recklessly. If you do not know the purpose and the sacredness of sex, you will give yourself to anyone. Sex is a gateway and it is not only a physical exchange, there is also a spiritual exchange when you are intimate with someone. In addition, with sex, you tie your soul to the one you are intimate with and just imagine not knowing the ramifications of soul ties or how to break them, you will be tied to partner after partner after partner and may wonder why when you get married, you have certain challenges that you cannot break from. God is awesome and everything about life and godliness, he gave us in his word. As we pray and seek him, he gives us insight about how to live.

Guard your sexuality young people, guard your sexuality. I never learned or knew about sex growing up and made a lot of mistakes that cost me a lot later in life. God intended for you to experience sex in marriage and not to fragment yourselves with different sexual partners. When you become intimate with someone, you give them a part of you, therefore, imagine how many ways you have broken yourselves up as you have had sex with different people. Please, don't do it. Popular culture is going to make you feel like an alien when you tell your friends you are saving your virginity for marriage. It may be a topic that you should probably not discuss with some of your friends as they may want to put added pressure on you and set you up to do what they are doing or have done. This is not about being afraid, you are not going to see the physical effects of making a Spiritual choice immediately. Spiritually, there is an exchange when you have sex with someone and later in life you wonder why you are having certain challenges. It may be because you have tied your soul with someone when you were a teenager or someone you are not married to and there are effects and consequences.

For instance, when you have sex with someone, pregnancy can be a real consequence. So, now a teenage boy is about to be a father and he is in the eleventh grade and has the responsibility of a man. He is to become a father when he has not gained the tools yet to be a man. For the young mother, now the thought of aborting the baby becomes a real option because she is not in a position financially and mentally to adequately care for a child that is supposed to be a blessing from God. When the situation is not ideal, it begins to seem like abortion is the only option. This situation of being pregnant when not ready is going to affect your education, the relationship with your parents, the relationship with your friends, and the relationship with the baby's father.

This can be a real stressor. Please, remember that life is a sacred gift from God. A child's life doesn't become irrelevant because the pregnancy wasn't planned. If you do not accept the fact that all life is sacred, then the enemy will allow you to choose to destroy one life or many more. The blood of that innocent soul will cry out and you will have to answer to God. The bible tells us that we should not kill and know that you will be held accountable. In his infinite mercy, if we repent, God is faithful and just to forgive us and cleanse us from all unrighteousness. This is not to make you feel guilty for anything you have done that you may think or know is not pleasing to God. It is to help equip you with tools so you can fulfill God's purpose for your life. Many things can get you side tracked when you are not enlightened and when you don't have God's knowledge and wisdom. Follow God's word, trust him and you will see things improve in your life.

You interconnect in sex and there is a physical and spiritual transfer once you join yourself with someone. That person transfers their demons to you, you do so to them. This is no conspiracy theory. You wonder why I say their demons, it is because the devil uses sex which God intended to be sacred, as a hinderance. It is a portal that can let spirits in. You meet a handsome boy as a teenager, and of course you don't know him well. When you interchange, you bind yourself with him and he becomes a part of you. Ok, it doesn't work out so you become intimate with another and bind yourself with that person and and another person and another. This is just an example of a teenage girl who may have had 5 sexual partners. Well why 5, because if there can be one, what stops it from being more than one when things don't work out. I see so many young people who have many challenges with demonic attacks being translated into mental health challenges, because of an open door through sexual activity.

This is because of some transfer that may have occurred. In the natural, it has to have a definition. In nursing school, you are taught about medical diagnoses, although the doctor is the one who diagnose diseases, not the nurse. Insurance companies do not pay for the origin of diseases, they pay for disease titles so we give titles. and labels. When you investigate, you see the origin and so much more makes sense. For instance, a teenage boy that is now being ignored by a young lady or vice versa, now feels worthless and hopeless because he no longer has her attention and wants to harm himself. That is an emotional consequence from an open door that came about by being intimate with someone that hasn't made a commitment in marriage. Now there is hurt and pain.

"My Christian mother never told me "I can't dictate the consequences of my actions."

Eleven

~

Well, everyone is doing it!

The teenage years can be very challenging and you may think you have to do what your friends are doing. That is a big problem because you do not know where they are getting their instructions from. As a Christian, your instruction must come from God's word and you usually get these instructions through your parents and your pastor. Let's be honest, as a teenager, you are amongst your peers, probably more than with your parents and you learn a lot from your friends. The problem with that is, if you have a non Christian friend, they probably don't have the same values and instructions as you do. What they learn from their parents as ok, may not be what you learn to be ok.

God has given you a unique opportunity to be a soul winner, not to be taken from light to darkness. The purpose of being in school is to get an education so please don't think you are missing out by not being a part of the popular crowd. One way to ensure you make good friends, is to always seek God's wisdom in prayer and ask for his will to be done in your life. The bible says, ask and you shall receive. You may have read about Solomon that asked God for wisdom. The bible also says that the "fear of the Lord is the foundation of wisdom.

and that knowledge of the Holy One results in good judgment" (Proverbs 9:10 NLT). Navigating your teenage years without God's wisdom can lead you wrong and cause you to walk in error. You know when you meet a friend at school and you get that feeling that you don't care for them or like them but you may not know why, it is because the holy Spirit talks to you when you have a relationship with him. That tiny voice that says do this or don't do this, can be the voice of the holy Spirit and you will know when it is him. The holy Spirit will not tell you what is not in line with the word of God.

Your friends are going to want you to try new things, talk in a way you know is out of your character or try to entice you. It is all a plan of the wicked enemy who is trying to lead you astray. The devil is not all knowing and he wants to lead you off the path that God has intended for you. Therefore, he is going to try to use people around you, people that have access to you. For instance, the devil is probably not going to talk to the president of a certain country to tell you to do something bad because what are the chances that president will every have an interaction with you and lead you astray. That is going to be highly unlikely because, due to your age, and due to his status, both of you would likely not have an opportunity to be in the same space, ever.

Now, as for your friends, they are the people you see always so you are likely to hear their ideas, but you do not have to accept their ideas into your Spirit. Some of the suggestions they present you are not merely coming from their head. It is a diabolical plan that the enemy is trying to present you. Darkness cannot put out light, only light can put out darkness. As the bible says we have been brought from darkness into God's marvelous light. When light shines, it dispels all darkness. You are the light of the world and others will want to be like you, when you walk in God's light. As a teenage, you may want to do or think you have to do what everyone is doing. You are going to be surprise that you are going to feel the same way as an adult. The same reason your parents may not be friends with people who do not have the same values, is the same reason you should do the same. Just because people are adults do not mean they have mastered the skills they should have at your age. When we are around others, we become like them. I cannot hang out in certain crowds because I do not want to make choices that may be detrimental to me.

That teenage boy or girl in detention does not get to choose the consequence for the action that caused them to end up in juvenile detention. How long they should be in Juvenile is not up to them but they must face their consequences. With the help of God, you can do all things through Christ which strengthens you. As a teenage, you have not had the opportunity to be exposed to life and for this reason, God has put your parents and your pastors, people in leadership and authority positions so they can guide you. We must be careful who we are around. As a behavioral health nurse, I get a unique opportunity to talk to teenagers on a regular basis that are going through major behavioral health challenges. God has not placed me in that position for no reason. As a teenager, God has placed you in a position to tell others about God's love and lead them into God's light, before things get bad for them. Your friends can learn from you and you can be a good example for them. You don't have to be a superstar to influence your peers.

By Virtue that you have a heart for God, he can use you, though he can use anyone he chooses to spread his word. What you will find is that even though you say no to your peers and your friends, they will still accept and respect you and if they don't then you know for sure, they are not friends God want you to have. It is important to test every Spirit as the Bible instructs us to do. Do not just become friends with people because they accept you. Know that you are unique and that you have a specific purpose in life that God intended for you.

You have intrinsic value and worth and if you know that, it is much easier to know it is ok to be your own best friend. Sometimes, make some positive affirmation statements such as

Affirmations
I am a child of the King
I have self worth
Is what I am doing pleasing God
Does this bring me closer to God
I am loved by God, no matter if I don't have friends
I am excellent
I have an excellent Spirit.
   You must know your own worth and know it doesn't come from your peers, it comes from within.

I, (place your name here), commit before God and heaven,
To saving myself for the right partner, I will not tie my soul or body until marriage.

"My Christian Mother never told me "to commit myself to God"

Twelve

～

God sees everything I do

As a teenager, it is important to be conscious of what you do and who you are around because those people mold you and help make you the person you become. As we talked about earlier, you are among your peers a lot and you may get to see what they do and who they are. Learn to separate yourself from those that do not walk with God. I mentioned that I talk to a lot of teenagers and I can give so many examples about the insight I have gained from teenagers over many years, including my own children. I recall talking to a young girl one day who discussed that she doesn't believe in God and that she has began to practice witchcraft. I was blown away. Another told me she is spiritual and when I asked her to elaborate, she said she builds alters and talks to her ancestors, her grand mother can call snakes and so many more demonic activities.

On the surface, it may seem cool and innocent but these behaviors can have real consequences that are detrimental. This is the reason it is important to stay in the word of God and learn things from God's perspectives. The devil doesn't want anything good for us so as innocent as witchcraft seem, it isn't and this young lady did not know she was opening a door into the Spirit world but not God's way. This is why it is important not to explore ungodly things because the devil doesn't give you anything for free. You will have to pay and not in a good way, if you involve yourself with demonic activity.

This means not exploring anything that the Bible disagrees with. You may have people in your school that talk about being gay and transgender and gender fluid and so much more. God is love and he teaches us to love everyone. You do not hate or treat anyone differently for any reason. That being said, you have the right to believe in the Bible and to believe in what the Bible says about sin and you present truth with love. You may be called homophobic, not because you treat anyone differently, but simply because of a difference of opinion. This can be merely due to a difference of values, morals, ideas and truth. Do not let anyone shame you because you do not believe what they do or agree with what they do and you should not shame anyone for the same or different reasons. The Bible teaches us to know sexuality is sacred between a man and a woman and the minute you tell others you do not agree or believe other ideas, then you may be accused of not being a Christian. Do not let others make you feel guilty because you are a Christian. As teenagers, your friends will challenge you, a boy may tell you that you must believe what they believe and you should call him a girl and use female pronouns like she or refer to him as them. Know that someone can believe what they want but they do not have the right to force their beliefs on you. This is why it is important to stay and know God's word so you can have an answer when they challenge you about why you believe what you believe.

Do not think as a Christian, you have to answer all the questions. You have the right to ask questions also and challenge others that do not believe what you believe. Don't let anyone make you feel guilty because of your beliefs. Don't celebrate sin, people are going to force you to say sin is ok but don't fall for it. Everything the Bible considers as sin, consider it as sin. Don't pick and choose so you can please your friends. Don't worry about winning an argument, worry about doing what the Bible says, because God sees everything we do. Some explanations may be above your reasoning but your belief in God is enough. The Bible says you owe no man anything but love. Only love. You do not owe your friends an argument or an agreement, you owe them love. Treat everyone the same and it doesn't mean you have to agree with them.

My Christian Mother never told me "it is ok to love all human beings and still disagree with them"

Thirteen

∽

sexually transmitted infections

Although God does not want us to use human wisdom, we can look at things from a human perspective and see the reason why we should use Godly wisdom. Diseases are a real thing and we can do our part in many areas to decrease our risk. The likelihood of contracting a sexually transmitted infection without physical contact is going to be almost none. In addition, drinking alcohol and driving may mean letting down your guards and doing something you did not intend to do. I have heard such stories so many times. We cannot justify wrong and no one has the right to take advantage of another. Despite that, we live in a wicked world and we cannot give the enemy any weapons that he can use to torment us. If a friend drinks, he or she may not be able to recall the events of a party and being drunk can result in them being taken advantage of.

This all started with taking a drink that can lead to drinking more than you intended and you may not even know when you have had too much to drink. This can also be the case when being sexually active. There are so many diseases that one can be exposed to and frankly, you run the risk of saying yes out of being pressured and you may not use protection which could result in pregnancy, disease or infection. During a discussion about abortion in which some teenagers were present, none of them understood why it is wrong and that life is sacred. No one taught them that if they did not make up their mind ahead of time, they may open themselves up to that option. The topic of rape and unplanned pregnancy came up. I explained to them about the sacredness of life. If you believe that life is sacred, then you believe that a person doesn't have the right to take another man's life. This has to be engraved in your hearts that a baby is a human being that you cannot just get rid off.

Their blood will cry out and that is an offense you will have to answer to God for. Since there is a chance of pregnancy when you have sex, that decision must be made that you will save yourself for marriage, not just for this reason, but because sex is sacred. A person may say well, if it happens, it happens. That is a dangerous game when it comes to sex because if you are not persuaded that sex is sacred, you run the risk of becoming intimate with multiple sexual partners and being entangled in a web of soul ties.

"My Christian mother never told me that God intended sex to be only within the sanctity of marriage as defined in the bible"

Fourteen

୰

God is love

Our Heavenly father is so full of love for us that he gave us the ultimate guide, his word, to help us excel in all things. He has the necessary design and the perfect plan to ensure we live a life that is pleasing to him but first, a life that is more beautiful and full of joy more than we could ever imagine. Our lives can be the perfect example of God's love in how we treat others. This means, being kind to others while not losing your self worth. We can be strong in our convictions as Christians and still contribute to society. In John 15:13 (NLT) it states that there is no greater love than to lay down one's life for one's friends. The bible shows us so many examples of God's infinite love towards us.

This is going to be an important part of how you navigate your teenage years, and ultimately, your life, when you put love at the center of everything you do. If you love your neighbor, you wouldn't steal from them. If you love your friend, your wouldn't hurt them. God wants us to walk in love and this doesn't mean that we cannot present truth. Being a Christian doesn't mean that you should accept everything and anything, especially when people misinterpret the Bible and tells you, oh you're a Christian, "so you should accept this or that". No matter what we face in life, know that you are loved and favored by God. He loves you so much that if you were the only one on earth, your life has enough worth for him to send Jesus Christ, his only son, Just to die so you can have eternal life.

God has given us instructions in his word, not to bully or just to tell us what to do. He loves you and wants the best for you. He has a perfect plan for your life and a purpose in life that only you can fulfill. You are not here by accident, nor are you reading this book just because, God wants you to walk in that purpose he has for you to achieve your goals and to live your best life in God. You may have many questions about if God is love, then why do people suffer. He loves u so much that he cares to instruct us and it is so clear to see his love, when you surrender your life to him and ask him to come into your heart.

The bible says who the Lord loves, he chastises. Just think about your own parents or the people that take care of you, can you image if they just allow you to do what you want to do. We need instructions and guidance in life. Would you really say your caregivers love you if they allow you to follow your own way that could lead you astray, without instructions? Allowing you to do what you want may include allowing you to go into harm's way. This is because you may not know it is a danger zone but as a parent who has wisdom and experience, they may know and caution you.

God is not giving you a sexually transmission infection because he wants to teach you a lesson but just think about it. You do not know a partner you are having sex with has gonorrhea or HIV and they do not want to tell you in fear of rejection, now you have contracted an infection that was not part of God's plan for you. Regardless of how we got where we are, God meets us in the midst of our needs and he beautifies our lives from where we are. He is so kind that he doesn't care what you have done or with who. If you confess your sins to him, he is faithful and just to forgive you. He doesn't hold your sins against you, not the ones you have committed, not the ones you are committing, and not the ones you will commit. Jesus Christ died for them all, so you can live.

Love does not keep track of wrong. When you come to God, he doesn't turn the pages back like humans do and remind you of how you hurt him. He wants to change your life because he loves you. What if you say, well, my life is great and I know God, this book is still a tool for you because the enemy is crafty, many teens do not start their teenage years making bad choices. Things may be going great and you may open a door to the enemy out of ignorance and the great life you have can begin to change. The devil loves people who considers themselves as self righteous so he can mess them us. Therefore, guard your heart and never open a door to the enemy, not through sex, through bad choices, through witchcraft, through disobedience to your parents and those that have been entrusted to care for you.

Lastly, never forget that no matter what, nothing can separate you from the love that God has for you. Romans 8:38-39 (NLT) states "for I am persuaded, that neither death, nor life, nor angels nor principalities, nor powers, nor things present, nor things to come, nor heights, nor depth, nor any other creature, shall be able to separate us from the love of God, which is in Christ Jesus our Lord". Amen.

As discussed earlier, body image is of great concern to some teens. They want to be liked and accepted by their peers especially. In the age of social media, having followers and friends mean something to them and it can affect their self image if they feel like they are not liked or accepted. I recently met a 12 year old beautiful girl who discussed being bullied in the past because of her height. She's a beautiful, 5'8 talented young lady. A negative body image can lead to body dysphoria (a mental health disorder in which you can't stop thinking about one or more perceived defects or flaws in your appearance) and unhealthy living. You are created in the image and likeness of the designer himself.

The bible says you are joint heirs with Christ. Just imagine the love of your heavenly father that cared about you in such a way that he printed his image on you. If you know the depth of what that means, you will have joy. This means that you will begin to see yourself through God's eyes. He loves you so much that he gave his best. He sent his son to die for us, so we can have life. Remember his image is on you so when you don't feel loved, know he loves you. When you don't feel happy, know joy comes from him. When you feel helpless or hopeless or sad or depressed, know he can make your life beautiful. I challenge you to tell yourself what you what to see about yourself. For instance, if you are sad, tell yourself "I am happy". Positive affirmations will help you change your thinking and help you with positive thought patters.

PRAYER

Dear Father,

Thank you for this wonderful opportunity to impact my world in a positive way. I am a soul winner and my life is for your works. Please guide me and help me make good choices in this complicated world. I am unique and I know you have a purpose for my life. I believe my sexuality is sacred and that life is sacred and I vow to protect both. I vow to save myself for marriage and protect my virginity. Thank you for being a good father, I love you in Jesus Name, Amen.

"My Christian mother never told me that even with prayer, we have a responsibility"

Fifteen

∽

"I commit"

God is awesome and everything about life and godliness, he gave us in his word. As we pray and seek him, he gives us insight about how to live. God has an amazing plan for your life. Your life is sacred and know that it has meaning and value given to you by no one but God. Live your life with boundaries. You must make a conscious decision to do so because if you do not, it becomes difficult to know what is meant to help you grow from what is meant to destroy you. Today, make a commitment to yourself and God to use your body and your mind for what it is intended.

I COMMIT

To saving myself for the right partner, I will not tie my soul or body to the wrong person

I will not become intimate with anyone until marriage.

I am (insert your name)

What I know is that I am created in the image and likeness of the designer himself

I am unique, enough and complete

I have all of my pieces and need no one to make me whole

I am genuine, honest and with integrity

I have the love of God and he guides me

I am divine, i'm noble, I'm loving and real

I am a soldier because I am steadfast about my cause

Most importantly, I am the Lord's and I refuse to believe otherwise! Amen.

"My Christian mother never told me my body is not a funhouse"

ABOUT THE AUTHOR

Envi is a Registered nurse and has been a nurse for over 20 years and currently serves as a Behavioral Health nurse. She received her Undergraduate degrees from the University of North Carolina at Charlotte (Bachelor of Arts in Biology) and from Winston Salem State University (Bachelor of Science in Nursing). In addition, she obtained a Master of Business Administration from Davenport University. She cares primarily for teens and preteens struggling with mental health challenges and frankly the pains of growing up in this fast and changing world. She's always had a heart for young people and God has given her a unique opportunity to share his love with these brilliant minds. Sometimes, just letting someone know God loves them is enough, no matter what they are going through. As a Christian, her goal is to not only assist and empower clinically, but also from a Spiritual perspective. Young people need to hear and know the truth, shared with them in a kind and loving way. May we have illumination by the power of the Holy Spirit.

www.ingramcontent.com/pod-product-compliance
Lightning Source LLC
Chambersburg PA
CBHW021955090426
42811CB00001B/34